PRE-COLUMBIAN DESIGNS
FROM PANAMA

591 ILLUSTRATIONS OF COCLÉ POTTERY

Samuel Kirkland Lothrop

DOVER PUBLICATIONS, INC.
NEW YORK

Published in Canada by General Publishing Company, Ltd., 30 Lesmill Road, Don Mills, Toronto, Ontario.

Published in the United Kingdom by Constable and Company, Ltd., 10 Orange Street, London WC 2.

Pre-Columbian Designs from Panama: 591 Illustrations of Coclé Pottery, first published by Dover Publications, Inc., in 1976, is a selection of illustrations from the work *Coclé: An Archaeological Study of Central Panama; Part II: Pottery of the Sitio Conde and Other Archaeological Sites* by Samuel Kirkland Lothrop, Vol. VIII of the Memoirs of the Peabody Museum of Archaeology and Ethnology, Harvard University, published by the Peabody Museum, Cambridge, Mass., in 1942.

(Part I of the work, not represented here, bore the part title *Historical Background; Excavations at the Sitio Conte; Artifacts and Ornaments*; it was published by the Museum as Vol. VII of its Memoirs in 1937.)

DOVER *Pictorial Archive* SERIES

International Standard Book Number: 0-486-23232-8
Library of Congress Catalog Card Number: 75-17177

Manufactured in the United States of America
Dover Publications, Inc.
180 Varick Street
New York, N.Y. 10014

PUBLISHER'S NOTE

Coclé is a province of central Panama on that nation's southern coast. Discoveries of Indian objects from Coclé were made sporadically from about 1850, but it was not until 1915 that a unified local culture of a high order was recognized by archeologists, and formal excavations began only in 1925.

Between 1930 and 1933 Harvard's Peabody Museum of Archaeology and Ethnology carried out extensive work in Coclé, the results of which were published in two large volumes in 1937 and 1942 (the latter also covering work done in 1940; for the full original titles, see the bibliographical statement on the facing page). The chief author of these books was the distinguished anthropologist Samuel Kirkland Lothrop (1892–1965), who directed the 1933 and 1940 excavations.

The Indian culture that created the unearthed objects was the one that was flourishing at the time of the Spanish Conquest in the early sixteenth century. These artifacts, which were found in burial sites, include objects of gold and other metals, jewelry of semiprecious stones, bone and ivory (whale-tooth) carvings, textiles and pottery.

The present book, which includes every illustration from the 1942 volume that shows a Coclé artifact, covers the pottery, which exists in a wide variety of forms and decoration. There are vessels with human heads, or in the shape of fish, frogs, birds, monkeys, coatis and other mammals. The painted motifs include striking geometric and abstract patterns, human and semihuman beings and many animal forms (birds, crabs, serpents, felines).

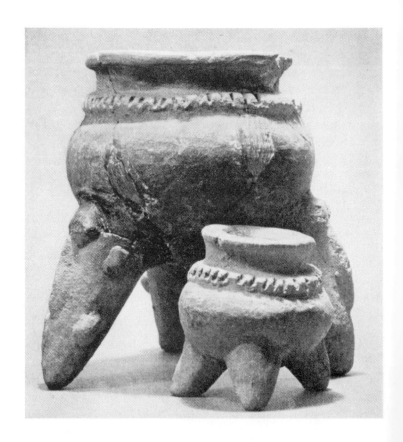

3

5

10

14

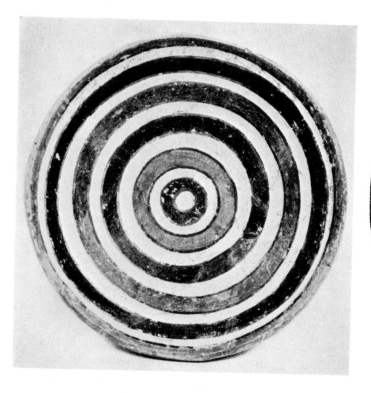

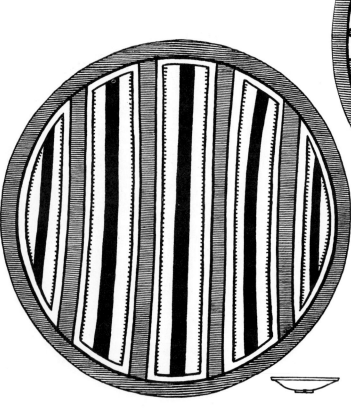

30

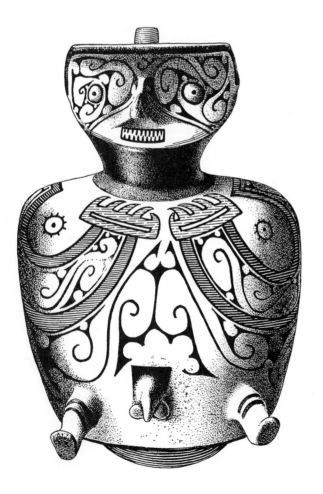

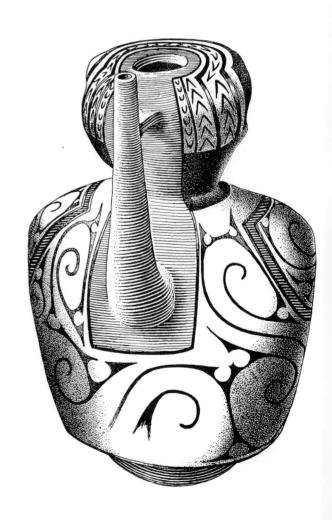

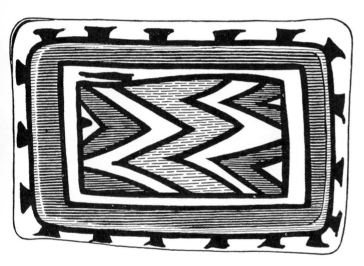

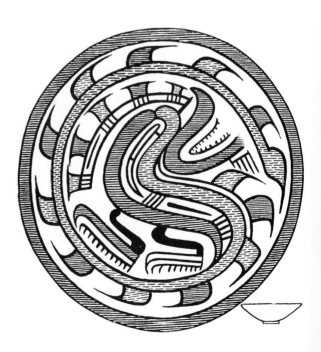

47

48

49

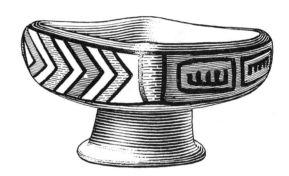

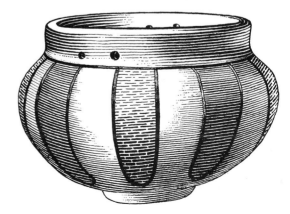

54

63

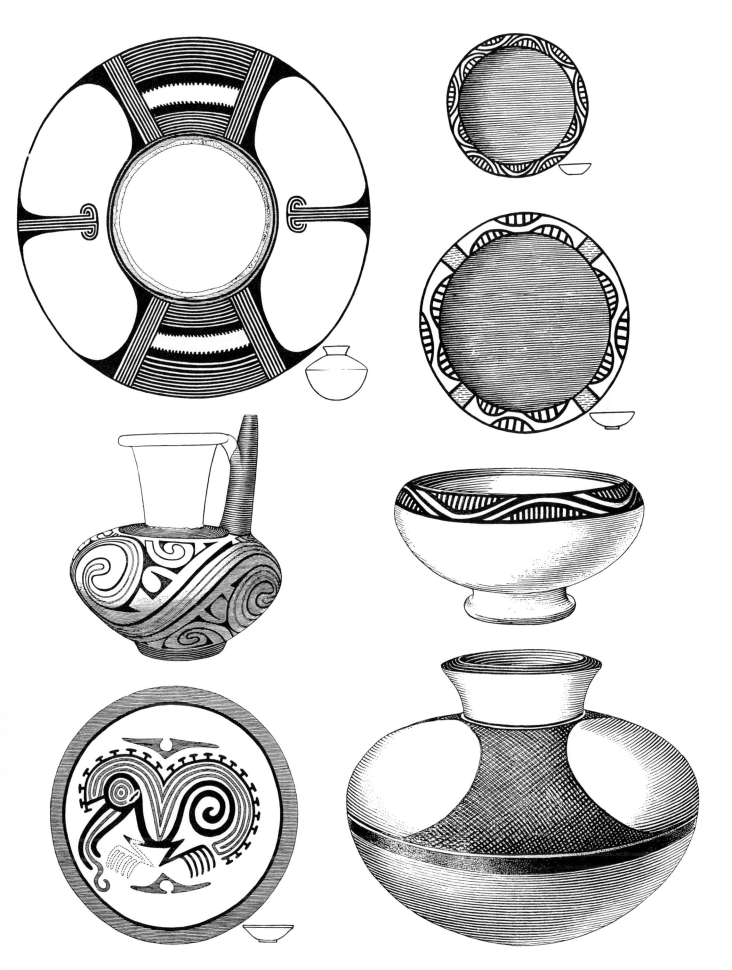

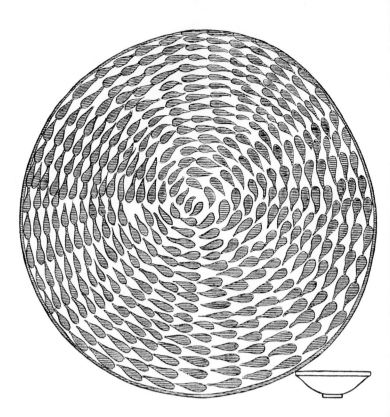

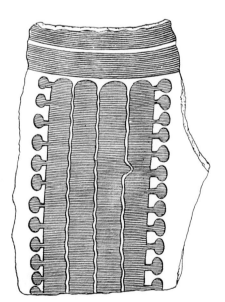

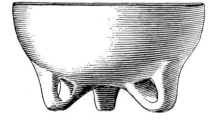

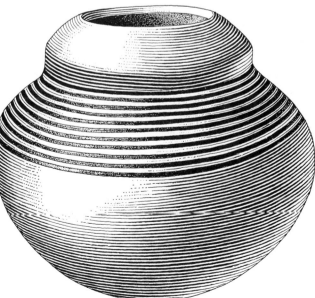

73

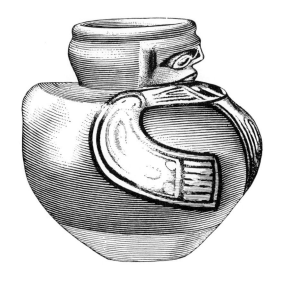

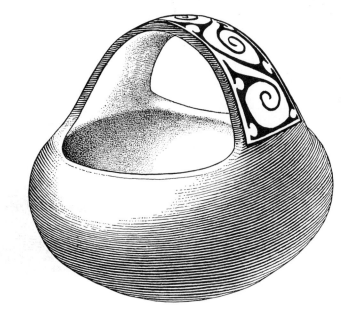

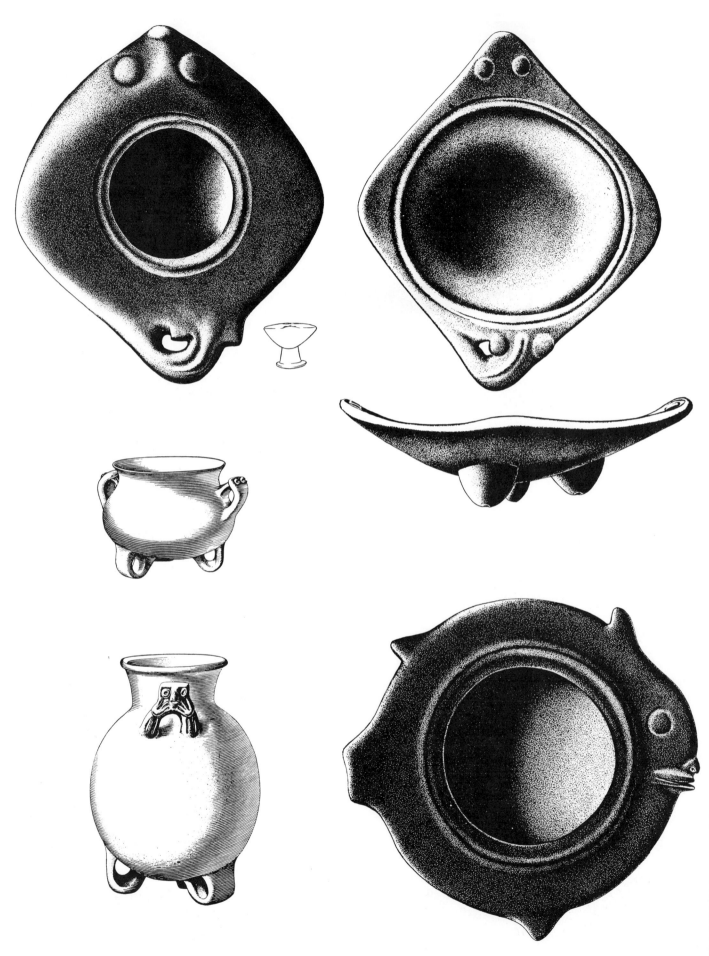

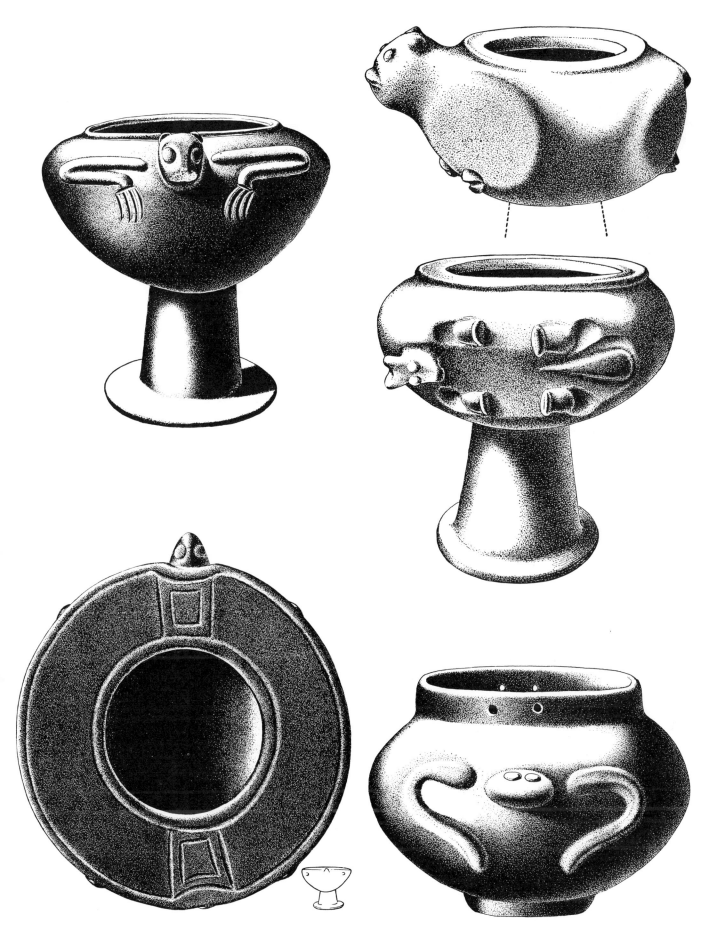

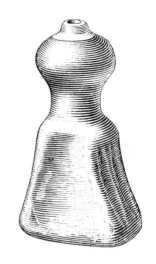

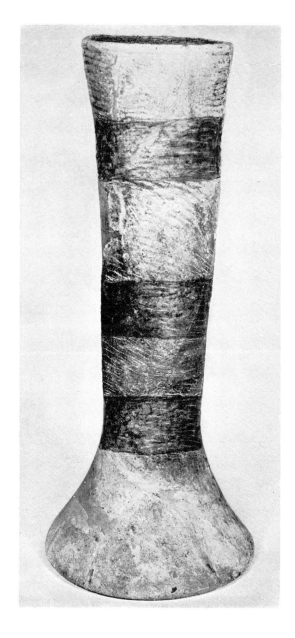

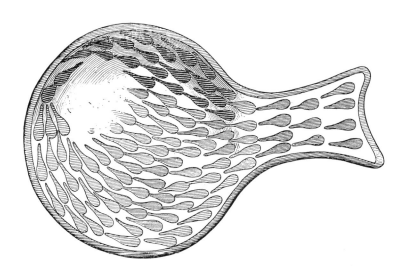

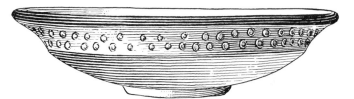

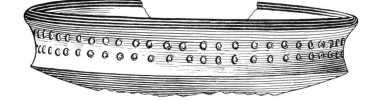

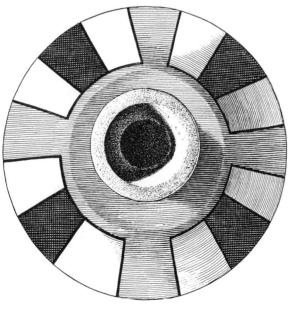

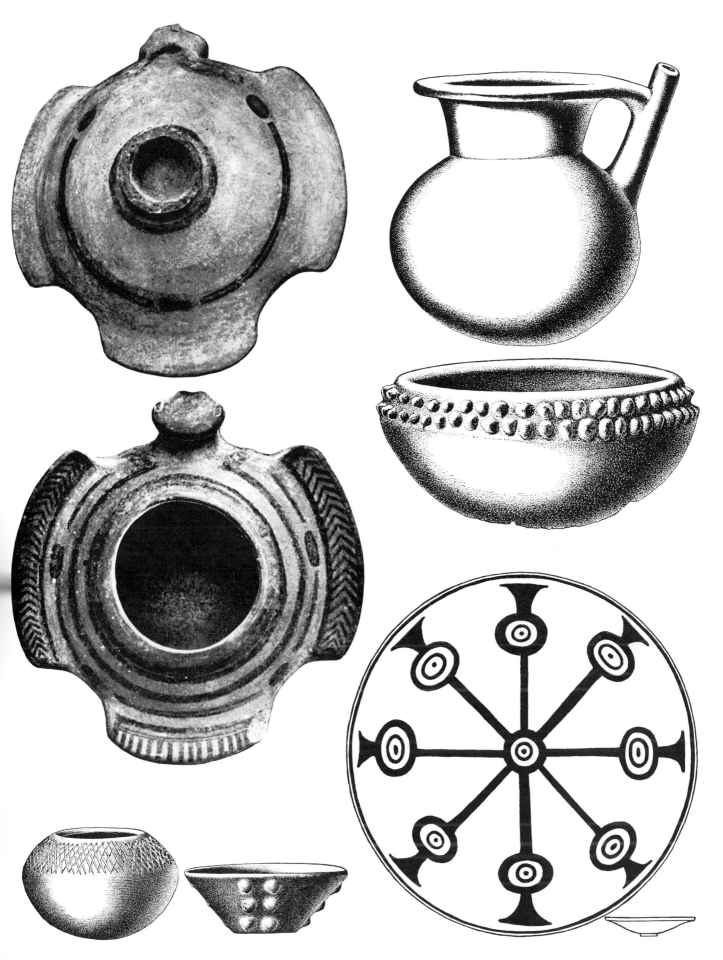

102

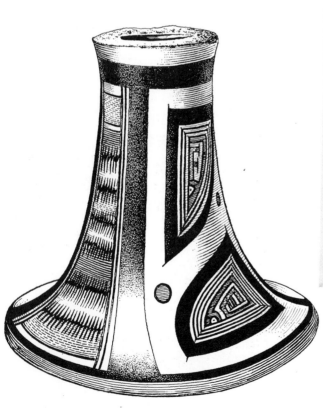